Anchor Counseling

Sex Offender
Treatment Program

James Robert Ross, Ph.D., LMFT
KY Certified Provider for Sex Offender Treatment (SORAAB No. 013)
Email anchor275@gmail.com

—revised August 23, 2020

Table of Contents

APPENDIX

Glossary (Definitions of Sexual Terms)

Introduction

The Anchor Counseling Sex Offender Treatment Program, assists sexual offenders in developing the maturity and acquiring the skills to prevent relapse and re-offending. The program does not provide a "cure." Clients are invited to assume responsibility for the pace and direction of their treatment by being offered a combination of both required and optional tasks.

The length of time necessary to complete treatment is determined by the success of the client in completing his or her Therapy Tasks. Two years is required by the regulations of the Commonwealth of Kentucky. Some clients may require longer. Progress depends, first, upon how the nature of the offense(s), and, second, upon the motivation of the client and how quickly he or she completes the required tasks. The program is based upon the premise that deviant sexual acts are rooted deeply in compulsive psychic processes that are seldom, if ever, eradicated. The sex offender should consider himself in recovery for life. If the client shows signs of an addiction (alcohol, gambling, or sex), he must participate in an adjunct 12 Step Program or meet with a 12 Step group. The three phases of the formal treatment program are (1) assessment and orientation, (2) therapy tasks, (3) and maintenance.

I - Assessment and Orientation
Psychosocial history
Psychological testing (if indicated)
Substance abuse and alcohol abuse assessment
Completion of a detailed Sexual History
Polygraph based on answers to a Comprehensive Sexual History
Meeting with a therapy partner
Completion of a satisfactory Layout/Basic Ownership by briefly answering these questions:

1. What crime did you commit? Describe specifically what you did.

2. What has been the effect on yourself judicially, financially, socially, and emotionally?

3. What has been the effect on your family and friends?

4. What has been the effect on your victim(s)?

5. Make a statement regarding your worth and dignity as a human being.

Phase II - Therapy Tasks
(1) Life and Sexual Autobiography
(2) Detailed Ownership of the Offense(s). The client should choose the task or tasks appropriate to his type of offense, which are:
      (i) Hands-On Offense and/or
      (ii) Child Pornography Offense and/or
      (iii) Voyeuristic or Indecent Exposure Offense
      (iv) Contact of a Minor for Sex

(3) Victim Empathy

(4) Relapse Prevention Strategies

(5) First Optional Task

(6) Second Optional Task

(7) Restitution

(8) Shame Resiliency

(9) Final Group Review

Phase III - Maintenance

Any client may be required to remain in maintenance for a period determined by his unique needs and/or the requirements of probation and parole. In the maintenance phase the client attends the therapy group on a less than weekly basis. He makes a Monthly Maintenance Report regarding his behavior. If he has an intimate sexual partner, he may also be asked to attend conjoint couple therapy.

Family Counseling and Family Reunification

Because of the importance of family attachment bonds to the victim, the goal of family reunification is important to the successful outcome of the treatment, especially in incest cases. Therefore, if and when the safety of the victim can be guaranteed, counseling with all members of the family including the non-offending spouse and siblings of the victim will address the issues which these members of the family face with the purpose of facilitating family reunification. If the client has a spouse or domestic partner and/or children, they may be required to participate in counseling as a couple and as a family either with the group therapist or with another therapist.

Treatment Objectives

ONE: Tell the truth, the whole truth and nothing but the truth.

A key factor in your treatment is learning to be completely honest and forthright, to always tell the truth, the whole truth and nothing but the truth. You must only disclose all past lies, deceptions, and previously undisclosed deviant behaviors. You must also learn to be honest about yourself at the present moment including either a fear or a desire or a fantasy regarding the pleasure of a deviant sexual act. Your ability to talk honestly about your sexual fantasies and desires will help you control or interrupt these fantasies and help you stop yourself from committing another deviant sexual act.

TWO: Recognize and accept sexual arousal including any deviant arousal.

Becoming aware of the psychological roots of your sexual behavior in your sexual fantasies is vitally important to your control of your behavior. In order to be able to implement relapse prevention strategies, which you will learn in treatment, you must recognize and own your sexual fantasies, which are a precursor to acting out.

THREE: Stop grooming or cruising behaviors.

You must learn to recognize and label your specific behaviors which have as their ultimate goal finding and cultivating a victim on whom you can safely (in your mind) commit your offense.

FOUR: Own *all* of your sexual offenses.

As long as you are hiding, denying, justifying or minimizing any offense you are vulnerable to a repetition of your sexual acting out. All offenses must not only be admitted, but you must also understand how hurtful they have been to your victims. We do not report any crimes you may have previously committed. However, we are required to report a current offense or any suspicion of an intent to commit an offense.

beyond this way of thinking. The goal is to stop justifying or minimizing your behavior and to accept full responsibility for it.

SIX: Develop empathy for your victim(s). Empathy is the ability to be sensitive to others' feelings, and as a sex offender you obviously need to learn to recognize and respond to others' signals of negative and positive emotions. Sex offenders have shown by their behavior that they are not sensitive to the feelings of their victims. Therefore, your treatment will focus upon helping you learn to understand what it is really like for a victim you have abused.

SEVEN: Develop and implement relapse prevention strategies.
There is a cyclical pattern to almost all behavior including sexual behavior. Treatment will help you understand this cycle and how you can develop a plan to interrupt it.

EIGHT: Develop a healthy shame resiliency.
Most offenders feel guilty. Without guilt there is no motivation to change. Most offenders also feel ashamed. Indeed, our society attempts to shame you in every possible manner. It is not reasonable that you, or any other person, should ever completely eradicate shame from his feelings. But shame can fuel destructive behaviors including sex offenses. Therefore, one objective of treatment is to help you become more resilient to shame and to liberate you from its most debilitating effects.

THERAPY TASK I - Life and Sexual Autobiography

Write an autobiography with as much detail as you can, especially about the most significant and formative events in your life. Your autobiography is not limited to the following subjects, but you must address all that apply to you. Emphasize the most formative events or phases in your life, that is, the parts of your life that seem to you to have had the most impact upon your life–both negative and positive. Look for and explain the connections between these formative events and your sexual offense.

In writing your autobiography follow the point by point out line below, and tell us about your:
(1) Early family life

> Relationships with parents–who were you closest to? With whom did you have the most conflict and why? Were you physically, sexually or emotionally?
> Your siblings and your relationships with them.
> The most painful memory or memories of your childhood.
> The best memories of your childhood.

(2) Education including academic success, sports, friends in school or behavior problems
(3) Military experience, if any
(4 Work experience including problems with employers
(5) Romantic relationships including, marriage(s), and divorces

> Did you date as a teen ager?
> Who was your first long term relationship
> What was the most difficult aspect of your intimate relationships?
> If married, tell us about your spouse: how you met, how you adjusted to marriage, any marital problems and how you handled them.
> If you have been through a divorce, tell us how it came about and how it affected your.

(6) Alcohol and drug history

> When did you start drinking or using drugs?
> How much did you use or how much did you drink?
> What problems did it cause in your life?
> Did you ever get help?

(7) Criminal offense history

> Trouble at school (suspensions or expulsions)
> Arrests including misdemeanors and felonies
> Convictions including misdemeanors and felonies

(8) Sexual experience including:

> How you learned about sex-when, where, from whom
> Your first sexual experiences
> How your family talked and felt about sex
> History of any sexual abuse
> Your first sexual partner-how was this relationship? Any unwanted pregnancy?
> Other sexual partners-how many?
> Your marriage(s) if any
> Sexual satisfaction today
> History of the use of pornography

(9) Spiritual development and religious life

THERAPY TASK II - Ownership
Introduction

You did not commit a sex offense because you simply wanted to do something bad or to commit a crime. When you committed your offense, you knew that it wrong to molest a child, rape an adult, expose yourself, view and/or distribute child pornography, or contact a minor for sex. But you committed the offense anyway? Why? What were you thinking that make it OK to do something that you knew was wrong?

You may say, "I wasn't thinking." But unless you were in a coma, you were conscious and were *thinking something*. You had some thought, perhaps vague and not openly expressed, that would make it right to do something wrong. Thoughts that justify or excuse a sex offense are called "thinking errors." Here is a list of some of the thinking errors that other sex offenders have used to justify, excuse or minimize their offense.[1] Which of these thinking errors did you use to justify your offense?

- ☐ I'll only do it one more time.
- ☐ I need to do this to reduce my tension.
- ☐ She/he likes it.
- ☐ She is too young to get pregnant/He can't get pregnant.
- ☐ She/he won't remember.
- ☐ She won't realize what I'm doing, she's too young/He's too young.
- ☐ Nobody will find out.
- ☐ I'm not really hurting, anyone.
- ☐ I'm just going to play around.
- ☐ At least I'm not having intercourse.
- ☐ She/he won't tell.
- ☐ She's not my real daughter/He's not really my son.
- ☐ My wife doesn't love me or give me the sex I deserve.
- ☐ It's okay since she's asleep/he's asleep.
- ☐ I'm just going to look, I won't touch.
- ☐ She's my daughter so its okay/It's okay, he's my son.
- ☐ He/she is better than no one at all.
- ☐ She wants love and affection.
- ☐ She/he likes being with me.
- ☐ We are very close friends.
- ☐ She/he likes attention.
- ☐ Women who behave and dress like that are just looking for sex.
- ☐ She/he didn't tell me to stop.
- ☐ Someone has to teach her/him about sex.
- ☐ I am lonely/bored.
- ☐ She/he wants me to do this.
- ☐ It makes me feel better.
- ☐ I need love and affection too.

---

[1] Adapted from Northwest Treatment Associates, 315 West Galer. Seattle, WA 98119

☐ She puts her arms around me or likes to sit on my lap.
☐ He/she says no, but really means yes.
☐ Women always like it rough.
☐ What does she expect dressed like that.
☐ Nobody is going to find out.
☐ She/he looks older than she/he is.
☐ She/he is very mature for his/her age.

Excuses for Child Porn Offenders
☐ It's just a picture.
☐ I was just curious.
☐ I'm just looking and not actually hurting the child.
☐ The kids were smiling.
☐ The child seemed to be enjoying it.

There are four basic types of sex offenses: hands-on offenses, child pornography offenses, and voyeuristic and/or indecent exposure offenses, and Contact of a Minor for Sex.

Part A: Hands-On Offense
Part B: Child Pornography Offense
Part C: Voyeurism and/or Indecent Exposure Offense
Part D: Contact of a Minor for Sex
Part E: Examination of Character Defects, which all clients must answer.

The client should complete his ownership for his own type of offense(s). Choose the task or tasks appropriate to your type of offense:

Part A: Hands-On Offense(s)
As you complete your ownership task describe exactly what you thought, felt and did as you committed your offense(s). The goal is to show 100% responsibility for your actions.

DO NOT use slang terms, or write about, or describe your victim's behavior to explain what happened.
DO NOT describe the victim's behavior except in answering No. 17(a).
DO use "I" statements. For example, "I fondled ... I forced ... I molested... I raped..."
DO Use correct anatomical terms, and focus on *your* behavior,

Use the point by point outline below in writing this task. Many of the assigned questions will give you some suggestions to help you prepare your answer for each point. However, you should not attempt to write about each point made by the suggestions unless they apply to you personally.

1. When was the very first time you thought of your victim in a sexual way? What were your first sexual thoughts about your victim(s). Describe in detail all of your sexual fantasies about your victim.

2. Identify and describe the Seemingly Unimportant Decisions (SUDs) you used as an excuse to enter your High Risk Situations whereby it would be possible or easy to commit your offense.

3. What was there about your victim(s) that seemed to invite your sexual approach?
    HERE ARE SOME SUGGESTIONS TO HELP YOU ANSWER THIS QUESTION:
Look first at any specific physical or personality characteristics about the person you victimized. Examples are lonely children seeming to be in need of affection or having the knowledge that an adolescent girl has already been sexually active. Did you see the other person as inviting your sexual approach? Did you pick this person because she/he happened to be available and vulnerable to your advances?

4. What was there about yourself that seemed to arouse your sexual interest in your victim?
    HERE ARE SOME SUGGESTIONS TO HELP YOU ANSWER THIS QUESTION:
Was your attraction to this person part of a general pattern of sexual attraction to similar persons, such as very young children or adolescent males? Describe your sexual fantasies about this person or similar persons. Was the vulnerability of your victim part of the attraction? Is there something about your character that made it possible for you to offend? Did you feel a need for power and control? Did you see yourself as providing missing love or affection to that person? Were there nonsexual motivations involved such as anger or personal unmet emotional needs?

5. What arousal enhancing activities, if any, did you participate in that increased your desire to offend against your victim(s)? Did you use pornography prior to your offense? How?

6. Define grooming and then tell how you groomed your victim(s). Include how you isolated, maneuvered, watched for an opportunity, plotted, planned, conned, tricked, etc.

7. Describe exactly what you did to what parts of the victim's body with what parts of your body. Describe precisely where and when you committed your offenses.

8. What went through your mind before you committed your offense? What did you tell yourself that made your behavior acceptable? (This is called a "thinking error.") If you have trouble remembering what you were thinking, make a guess as what you might say to yourself to make it ok to commit your offense(s).

9. What emotions did you feel before and during your offense? Describe the excitement from the thrill of taking a risk and doing something wrong.

10. Describe how you were able to get your victim to do what you wanted him/her to do. Did you force or threaten or use a weapon? Did you use sweet talking, playing, buying gifts, tricking, or lying? Or did your victim go along with you without any resistance? If so, why do you think he or she did not resist?

11. What did you say to your victim(s) during the assault, and what did you make your victim(s) say while you were assaulting them?

12. If you committed more than one offense, what rituals or patterns did you follow when offending?

13. Describe how you kept the secret. What did you say to keep the people you abused and/or others from telling about your offense?

14. Identify and describe in detail all of the excuses and rationalizations you used to justify and excuse your sexual crimes.

15. Just before you offended describe your fantasy about what the offense would be like before you offended (a) for yourself and (b) for your victim.

16. Just after you offended or while you were actually committing the offense, describe what it was actually like. Was the actual act different from what you thought it might be like (a) for you. and (b) was it different for your victim than what you imagined? If so, how?

17. Describe the consequences, not for yourself, but for the following people:
- your victims,
- the victims' family and friends, and
- your own family and friends

18. Finally, answer the questions in **Part E: Examination of Character Defects**

Ownership
Part B: Possession/Distribution of Child Pornography

As you complete this task use the point by point outline to describe exactly what you thought, felt and did as you committed your offense. The goal is to show 100% responsibility for your actions.

DO NOT (1) use slang terms, or (2) write about or describe your victims behavior. **DO** (1) Use correct anatomical terms. (2) Describe exactly what you viewed (and distributed) and what sex acts were being performed, by whom and upon whom. (3) Describe your own arousal and whether you masturbated to the images you viewed.

Use this point by point outline below in writing this task.
1. When did you first begin to think of children in a sexual way? What were your first sexual thoughts about your victim(s). Describe in detail all of your sexual fantasies about children.

2. Do you have sexual fantasies of children when you are not viewing a picture of a child? If, "yes," how did these fantasies begin and when are you most likely to have these fantasies?

3. Do you masturbate to child pornography offline? If, "yes," how often and when are you most like to masturbate to fantasies of minors?

4. Have you ever been in contact with a minor with whom you communicated online? Explain.

5. Did your use of the internet create more interest in child pornography? Explain.

6. Which of the following have you done?

_____ Just viewed child porn without downloading any images.

_____ Viewed and downloaded images of child porn.

_____ Masturbated to images or to a fantasy of a minor

_____ _____ Collected as much child porn as I possibly could.

_____ Sent some child porn pictures to others.

_____ Became very active in a child porn group online, receiving and sending messages.

7. When you were most active how often did you view child porn:

_____ Daily

_____ Weekly

_____ Every few weeks

8. What benefits did you receive from child porn? (Check all that apply.)

_____ Sexual gratification

_____ Escape from feeling lonely

_____ Felt wanted and needed

_____ Escape from family conflict

9. Identify and describe the Seemingly Unimportant Decisions (SUDs) you used as an excuse to enter your High Risk Situations whereby it would be possible or easy to commit your offense.

10. What is there about your child victims that seems to invite your sexual fantasies about them? HERE ARE SOME SUGGESTIONS TO HELP YOU ANSWER THIS QUESTION: Look first at any specific physical or personality characteristics about the children. Examples are lonely children seeming to be in need of affection or thinking about children or adolescents already being sexually active. Did you or do you see the children as inviting a sexual approach?

11. What was there about yourself that seemed to arouse your sexual interest in children? HERE ARE SOME SUGGESTIONS TO HELP YOU ANSWER THIS QUESTION: Was your attraction to children part of a general pattern of sexual attraction to children? Describe all your sexual fantasies about the children you viewed on pornography. Did you feel a need for power and control? Did you see yourself as providing missing love or affection to children? Were there nonsexual motivations involved such as anger or personal unmet emotional needs?

12. What arousal enhancing activities, if any, did you participate in that increased your desire to look at child pornography?

13. What went through your mind before you viewed child porn? What did you tell yourself that made your behavior acceptable? (This is called a "thinking error.")

14. What emotions did you feel before and during your offense? Was there some excitement from the thrill of taking a risk and doing something wrong.

15. If you committed more than one offense, what rituals or patterns did you follow when offending?

16. Describe how you kept the secret. What did you say to keep the people you abused and/or others from telling about your offense?

17. Identify and describe in detail all of the excuses and rationalizations you used to justify and excuse viewing child porn.

18. End your Ownership Task by describing the consequences not for you but for the following people. Guess if you have to.
- your victims,
- the people in the victims' lives, and
- your own family and friends

19. Finally, answer the questions in **Part E: Examination of Character Defects**

Ownership
Part C: Voyeurism and/or Indecent Exposure Offense
As you complete this task use the point by point outline to describe exactly what you thought, felt and did as you committed your offense. The goal is to show 100% responsibility for your actions.

> **DO NOT** (1) use slang terms, or (2) write about or describe your victims behavior.
> **DO** (1) Use correct anatomical terms. (2) Describe exactly when, where and how you committed your offenses.

Use this point by point outline below in writing this task.

1. When did you first begin to think about peeping or exposing yourself?

2. What sexual fantasies did you have when peeping or exposing yourself.

3. When was your first offense? How many times have your committing your offense in your lifetime? When was your last offense?

4. Did you masturbate when peeping or exposing yourself?

5. Was there any special type of victim to whom you exposed yourself or whom you wanted to see?

6. Were you ever caught peeping? If so, what happened?

7. If you exposed yourself, what was the reaction of your victims?

8. What patterns of behavior did you use in committing your offenses?

9. How often did you offend?

    ____Daily

    ____Weekly

    ____Every few weeks

10. What benefits did you receive from your offenses? (Check all that apply.)

    ____Sexual gratification

    ____Escape from feeling lonely

    ____Felt wanted and needed

    ____Escape from family conflict

11. Identify and describe the Seemingly Unimportant Decisions (SUDs) you used as an excuse to enter your High Risk Situations whereby it would be possible or easy to commit your offense.

12. What was there about yourself that seemed to arouse your sexual interest in peeping or exposing yourself? HERE ARE SOME SUGGESTIONS TO HELP YOU ANSWER THIS QUESTION: Did you feel a need for power and control? Did you see yourself as giving your victim a sexual thrill? Were there nonsexual motivations involved such as anger or personal unmet emotional needs?

13. What arousal enhancing activities, if any, did you participate in that increased your desire to offend? Describe the history of your use of pornography.

14 What went through your mind before you offended? What did you tell yourself that made your behavior acceptable? (This is called a "thinking error.")

15. What emotions did you feel before and during your offense? Was there some excitement from the thrill of taking a risk and doing something wrong.

16. Identify and describe in detail all of the excuses and rationalizations you used to justify and excuse your offenses.

19. End your Ownership Task by describing the consequences not for you but for the following people. Guess if you have to.

        (a) your victims,

        (b) the people in the victims' lives, and

        (c)your own family and friends

20. Finally, answer the questions in **Part E: Examination of Character Defects**

Ownership
Part D: Contact of a Minor for Sex

As you complete this task use the point by point outline to describe exactly what you thought, felt and did as you committed your offense. The goal is to show 100% responsibility for your actions.

DO NOT (1) use slang terms, or (2) write about or describe your victims behavior.

DO (1) Use correct anatomical terms. (2) Describe exactly what you said or did. (3) Focus on your behavior.

Use this point by point outline below in writing this task.

1. When did you first begin to think of minors in a sexual way? What were your first sexual thoughts about a potential victim? Describe in detail all of your sexual fantasies about minors.

2. Did you ever masturbate to a fantasy of a minor? If, "yes," how often and when are you most likely to masturbate to fantasies of minors?

3. Explain how and when your were in contact with a minor.

4. Did your use of the internet create more interest in sex with a minor? Explain.

5. Which of the following have you done?
    _____ Just chatted with a minor using sexualized language.
    _____Viewed and downloaded images of child porn.
    _____ Arranged to meet a minor for sex.
    _____ Sent some sexual pictures to a minor.
    _____ Received some sexual pictures from a minor.
    _____ Masturbated to a fantasy of a minor.

6. When and for how long were you active in chatting with a minor about sex?

7. What benefits did you receive from these sexual contacts with a minor? (Check all that apply.)
    _____Sexual gratification
    _____Escape from feeling lonely
    _____Felt wanted and needed
    _____Escape from family conflict

8. Identify and describe the Seemingly Unimportant Decisions (SUDs) you used as an excuse to enter your High Risk Situations whereby it would be possible or easy to commit your offense.

9. What is there about your child victims that seems to invite your sexual fantasies about them? (SUGGESTIONS TO HELP YOU ANSWER THIS QUESTION: Look first at any specific physical or personality characteristics about the children. Examples are lonely children who seem to need affection or minors who are already sexually active. Did you or do you see the children as inviting a sexual approach?)

10. What was there about yourself that seemed to arouse your sexual interest in children? (SUGGESTIONS TO HELP YOU ANSWER THIS QUESTION: Was your attraction to children part of a general pattern of sexual attraction to children? Describe all your sexual fantasies about the children you viewed on pornography. Did you feel a need for power and control? Did you see yourself as providing missing love or affection to children? Were there nonsexual motivations involved such as anger or personal unmet emotional needs?)

11. What arousal enhancing activities, if any, did you participate in that increased your desire to have sex with a minor?

12. What went through your mind before you contacted a child about sex? What did you tell yourself that made your behavior acceptable? (This is called a "thinking error.")

13. What emotions did you feel before and during your offense(s)? Was there some excitement from the thrill of taking a risk and doing something wrong?

14. If you committed more than one offense, what rituals or patterns did you follow when offending?

15. Describe how you kept the secret of your contacts with minors about sex. What did you say to keep the children and/or others from telling about your offense?

16. Finally, complete **Part E: Examination of Character Defects.**

Ownership
Part E: Examination of Character Defects

All clients must answer these questions. What was there about your character that made it possible for you to offend? Check all of the character defects described below that apply to you:

☐ Self Centered: Thinking only of your personal needs without regard for others.

☐ Entitlement: Feeling that you are entitled and deserve what you want, when you want it, no matter how it affects anyone else.

☐ Phoniness: Presenting yourself as someone you are not.

☐ Impatience: Getting irritable or angry when things don't happen as fast as you like or the way you want to.

☐ Resentful and angry: Carrying around lots of anger; touchy and irritable.

☐ Irresponsibility: Not paying your bills, picking up after yourself, letting someone else do what you ought to do and blaming others for your own failures.

☐ Arrogance: Believing and acting like you are superior to others and deserve special treatment.

☐ Dishonesty: Willing to lie or cheat to make things easier for yourself.

☐ Self pity: Looking upon yourself as a mistreated victim.

☐ Show off: Acting loud, crude or vulgar in order to get attention from others.

☐ Controlling: Wanting to have your own way and willing to argue, manipulate or use anger to get your way.

☐ Envy: Jealous of what others have and resentful of their good fortune.

☐ Judgmental: Quick to find fault with others.

Describe how each of these character defects which your checked contributed to your committing your offense(s).

THERAPY TASK III - Victim Empathy

The Victim Empathy Task has three parts: (1) Learning the effect of sex abuse on the victim, (2) putting yourself in your victims "shoes," expressing a deep understanding of what it was like for your victim to be abused by you, and (3 an apology letter.

Before beginning this task, study and familiarize yourself with the following information on problems experienced by victims of sexual abuse. Not every victim suffers from all of the problems listed below. Every victim is an individual and will respond to his or her abuse in an individual way. The description of these problems, however, has been compiled by the reports of and observation os many, many victims. All victims experience some combination of problems, and most will suffer some symptoms from each of the broad categories listed.

As you read about the effect of sex abuse on victims, you should make notes to help you write your essay "What I Learned about the Effect of Sex Abuse on the Victims"

Self-Esteem and Self-Image

Sexual abuse makes people feel like "used property" or "damaged goods". They may feel "bad", "sinful", or "evil". This is because they often assume that the abuse was in some way their fault. They may think, "I shouldn't have trusted you, looked so attractive, or I must have done something wrong to bring this upon myself." Victims are often left with a sense of no personal power or control of their life. They feel they cannot protect themselves or their loved ones around them. The may be a sense of shame about his or her body, especially if there was any physical arousal that occurred during the attack. This is especially true for sexually abused children because their sense of self worth is just developing. Also, sexually abused children are often those who already have low self-esteem which makes them easy targets for sexual assault by an adult.

Some of the long-term problems include:

- Feeling ugly inside.
- Feeling worthless.
- Feeling that they are in the way.
- Being overly submissive and anxious to please.
- Feeling that they are stupid, a failure, a loser.
- Guilt and shame.
- A tendency to blame themselves for whatever goes wrong.
- An inability to concentrate and complete tasks successfully.
- A tendency to sabotage their own successes—victims may not believe they deserve success or anything good happening to them.
- A tendency to be victimized by others. This is particular y true for children who have learned that one way to get attention from adults is through sex. Also, they come to believe that they deserve to be victimized and ow people to walk all over them in a variety of ways.
- Feelings of helplessness.

Relationship Problems

Most victims report some form of relationship problems after being abused. The offender is often someone the child loved and trusted. The offender betrays this trust by lying, coercing, and manipulating the child into doing things that hurt, humiliate, and frighten the child. It is no surprise that child victims have a difficult time as adults trusting others. Because the relationship with the perpetrator was based on manipulation, deception, lies and secrecy, a terrible foundation is established on which to build later relationships. Women who have bee raped report intense feelings of fear of getting close to others. They fear physical injury, mutilation, and death. These feelings color their emotions and reactions to others in the future, particularly men. They become cautious with all people. They may be overly irritated and feel that no one understands them.

Some of the long-term problems in personal relationships include:
- Difficulty trusting others.
- Being distant and aloof. A deep sense of isolation-
- A tendency (especially among abused children) to get involved with destructive people who abuse them physically, verbally, emotion , or sexually.
- A lack of empathy or concern for others. Victims may be so concerned with their own survival that they are unable to reach out or notice other people's problems, even their own children.
- Difficulty with physical affection; not wanting to be touched or hugged. An inability to express physical affection. A fear of the motives of others or being misunderstood when they are affectionate.
- Secrecy, evasiveness, and a tendency to withhold personal information from others. Sometimes children who have been sexually abused have the opposite reaction and have a tendency to "tell all" even when it is inappropriate. This reflects a lack of personal boundaries.
- Child sexual abuse victims have a tendency to try to buy love. They may help others so much that they become exhausted, depriving themselves in order to give to others. They may give away personal possessions or have sex with anyone who desires them just to be liked.
- Difficulties with authority figures like bosses, teachers, car leaders who may remind them of the abuser.
- Difficulty communicating one's personal desires, thoughts, and feelings to others.
- Difficulty receiving from others. This includes awkwardness in accepting presents, favors, or compliments. They feel they are dirty and unworthy. Sometimes the opposite may occur where they expect others to show them love by buying presents or giving money. This may be particularly true of child victims who were showered with gifts and toys by the molester as a ploy to gain trust and positive feelings so the child could be molested.

Physical Problems

Because a sexual assault is against the body, victims frequently suffer from a series of psychologically based physical illnesses. In addition, their bodies continue to give them important messages about what the abuse was like and what their bodies need now in order to heal.
Long-term problems may include:
- Migraine headaches.
- Bladder and vaginal infections.
- Skin disorders.
- Numbness or tingling in the legs or arms.
- Frequent sore throats. Difficulty swallowing.
- Unexplained vaginal pain.
- Unexplained rectal and anal pain. Frequent stomach upsets.
- General pain in the muscles and joints.
- Changes in the menstrual cycle.
- A tendency to be accident prone. Victims may unconsciously punish themselves.

Sexual Problems

Sexual crimes often they result in long-term sexual problems for the victim. For children, this may be their first sexual experience. Instead of being and experience of love and tenderness, this initiation was one of exploitation and violence. Because of the early age of sexualization it can very difficult for the victims to later distinguish between love and sex. Almost all victims have difficulty making their adult sexual relations a positive experience. Instead, sex brings with it fear, pain, and anger. Each new sexual encounter may be accompanied by memories and flashbacks of the abuse and the abuser.

Some of the long-term problems may include:

- Lack of sexual desire or inhibition of sexual feeling (i.e., frigidity).   Inability to enjoy sex or to have an orgasm.
- Or the exact opposite: sexual promiscuity. The victim may become sexually promiscuous and see herself as having value only for sex, especially if she identified the sex abuse as a child as the only way to get approval and affection.
- Attraction to illicit sexual activities such as pornography or prostitution.
- Sexual dysfunctions. For females this may include vaginismus, an involuntary contraction of the vaginal muscles making intercourse difficult or impossible. For males, this may include problems in achieving or keeping erections (impotence).
- Inability to enjoy certain types of sexuality (fear of penetration or of being touched on certain parts of the body, etc.).
- Problems with sexual identity. This may be particularly true for boys who have been abused who may question their masculinity or who may be conflicted about being gay.
- Feeling that all sex is dirty and should be avoided.
- Anger and disgust at any public display of affection, sex, or nudity.
- Feeling that sex is a way to manipulate people and get w at you want in your social, marital, or business relationships. Sexualizing all relationships or thinking that all relationships must include sex.
- Sexual addiction or coping with anxiety and unpleasant feelings by promiscuous sex, compulsive masturbation or the use of pornography.

Emotional Problems
Victims have difficulty understanding, acknowledging, and expressing their emotions. They feel overwhelmed by their feelings. Many victims suppress their emotions, which results in severe depression. Other victims have a difficulty controlling feelings like anger, and may become violent towards others or abusive toward themselves. Long-term emotional problems may include some of the following:

- Intense anger and rage that sometimes bursts out unexpectedly.
- Mood swings, ranging from deep depression to an over active excited state.
- Chronic depression, resulting in sleeping too much and f ling listless, helpless, hopeless, and even suicidal.
- Dissociation, the experience of not feeling a part of oneself Often victims report severe memory lapses. Others report that it was as if they were outside of their bodies watching themselves during the abuse. They get a far away look in their eyes as if they are somewhere else. This comes from an emotional protection mode to the devastation of the sexual abuse.
- Irrational fears. This may include a fear of leaving home, going to the dentist, taking a bath or shower, or falling asleep.
- Sleep disturbances such as nightmares, not being able to sleep through the night.
- Addiction to food, alcohol, or drugs. These serve as a anger, pain, and fear.
- Obsessive thoughts or compulsive behavior such as or excessive cleaning. These are ways that victims anxiety.
- Eating disorders such as anorexia (slowly starving themselves) or bulimia (compulsive over-eating and purging)
- Flashbacks or hallucinations where the victim is suddenly flooded with memories of the abuse. These are usually triggered by something that reminds the victim of the abuser.

These flashbacks are associated with a sense of panic, dizziness, feeling sick to their stomach, or fear.

- Abusive behavior towards others. This may include lying, stealing or sexually abusing others. Victims can become victimizers of others.
- Self-destructive behavior. The rate of suicide among sexual abuse victims is much higher than for the general population. Other self-destructive behavior includes prostitution, and self-mutilation such as cutting or burning oneself.

Part One: What I Have Learned about the Effect of Sex Abuse on My Victims

Write an essay on what you have learned from reading the above description of the effects of sex abuse upon their victims.

Part Two: Putting Yourself in Your Victim(s) Place

Your recovery depends upon your ability to empathize with your victims, including the victims in child pornography. Empathy is the ability to exchange places with the person/persons you abused and feel what your victims felt. Among the purposes of this assignment is to make you aware of the pain and damage you inflicted upon your victim(s). If you do not have direct information from your victim, study the information above on problems experienced by victims and use your imagination to help you complete your victim empathy task.

Write a detailed first person essay using the pronoun "I" and write from the perspective of the person(s) you abused. Write a first person account beginning with the words "I felt" to describe how your victim(s) felt as he/she went through all the following aspects of the ordeal of enduring the offense you committed against them. If you have viewed child pornography, write your essay from the point of view of one of the children in the pictures you viewed.

1. Describe how you, the victim, experienced your **relationship with the perpetrator** before the offense. Was your perpetrator good to you? Had you developed a trust in him or her?

2. Describe how you, the victim, felt and acted **during the grooming phase** of your offense. What were some the first things he/she did or said that made you feel uncomfortable or wonder what was happening?

3. Describe how you, the victim, felt **during the actual offense**. (The perpetrator should put himself in his victim's shoes. Write in the first person, present tense, as if you are the person and the offense is happening now. Describe how you believe the victim probably felt during the offense.

4. Describe how you, the victim, felt **immediately following** the rape, molestation or assault (physical assault or visual assault). What were the predominant emotions experienced by your victim?

- Your victim's experience and feelings in the emergency room or during the medical exam–if this actually happened.
- If relevant your victim's experience of the interview by police or social worker.
- Your victim's experience and feelings at the time of the trial if there was one.

5. Describe the long term effect (five to twenty years from now) your offense has had or likely will have on you, the victim. What life-long trauma or damage was inflicted on your (a) emotional and mental health, (b) your self perception and self esteem, and (c) your relationships?

Write in the first person present tense, e.g., "Its been ten years since I was raped; I have nightmares and I am scared of being in the dark."

6. How did your offense effect your victim's family, friends and loved ones? How did they cope with the news of what you had done to your victim?

Part Three: The Apology Letter

Write an apology letter to the person/persons you abused. The purpose of the apology is not to make the victim feel better or to forgive or accept you. The purpose is for you to express your responsibility and accountability for your behavior. You should not ask your victim to "understand" or to "forgive." These are the components to a good apology:

(1) **A**ddress the victim directly

(2) **A**void "if," "but" and "maybe."

(3) **A**dmit your specific offiense

(4) **A**cknowledge the hurt you have caused.

(5) **A**ccept the consequences.

(6) **A**lter your behavior.

NOTE: Do not send your letter of apology until it has been approved and accepted by the group, and do not send it if you are ordered to have no contact with your victim(s).

THERAPY TASK IV- Relapse Prevention

There are four parts to this task: (1) An explanation of important terms used to understand and explain what happens in a relapse cycle, (2) A diagram and explanation of your personal relapse cycle, (3) a explanation of the Three Steps To Healthy Coping and (4) The completion of the *Relapse Prevention Workbook for Sexually Compulsive Behaviors*.

Part One: Understanding and Explaining How a Relapse Occurs

(1) Antecedent Factors: Describe the antecedent factors that put you at risk to commit an offense. These factors refer to aspects of your personality, character defects, your life experience and your current situation that contributed to your being able to commit your offense. These factors can include beliefs, such as a sense of entitlement to sex on demand from your partner. They can also include vulnerabilities or personal problems, such as a poor self image or inability to ask directly for what you need from others. Situational factors are those events and circumstances that occurred shortly before your offense. Examples include being in an unhealthy relationship, the loss of a partner, or being fired from a job; in short, an event or ongoing situation that you found stressful or traumatic.

(2) Deviant Sexual Fantasies: Describe the kind of deviant sexual fantasies you were having before your offense. Do not leave anything out. Describe who was in your fantasies and what you said and did to them. Describe how your victim responded to you as your fantasized about the abuse. How did your fantasies end? Explain why your fantasies are deviant and the role they played in your sexual offenses. Describe what the assault was really like and how it was different from your fantasies for the person you abused.

(3) Disinhibitors: Disinhibitors are those things which facilitated your decision to cross boundaries, to intrude sexually on the other person. Examples of disinhibitors include alcohol and drugs, use of pornography, attending strip clubs, and anything else that contributes to a distorted view of human sexuality. What were some of your disinhibitors? Explain the effect of each on your behavior.

(4) Thinking Errors: Define thinking errors for the group. What role did they play in your offending? Give examples of the types of thinking errors you employed to excuse, alibi, justify and rationalize your abusive behavior. How have you presented your offense to make the abuse seem not so bad, less serious, or less harmful? Include the small, seemingly unimportant, subtle ways that you minimize your offense(s) to family, friends, the group and yourself. How have you used minimization to protect yourself and how has it hampered you in your recovery. Tell us how you will correct these thinking errors. Finally, identify some of the ways you have heard members of your group minimize their offenses.

(5) Grooming: Define grooming. What role did it play in the sexual abuse cycle? Describe the grooming techniques used on your victim. Identify the subtle thinking errors you used to minimize, justify, excuse, and disguise your grooming. Correct these thinking errors. Is it possible to groom yourself? How?

(6) High Risk Situations, Warning Signs and Triggers: Define high risk situations, warning signs and triggers without using notes. Describe what role they played in your sexual abuse cycle. Identify and list your own high risk situations. Describe how you will deal with these high risk situations without committing an offense. Give one example of how others might encourage you to enter a high risk situation. Describe how you would avoid each one. List two thinking errors that you use to place yourself in a high risk situation. Correct these thinking errors.

(7) Reentering Your Cycle: You may have committed multiple offenses or you may have repeatedly victimized the same person or persons. You may have abused several different people. You possibly even committed a variety of different sexual offenses with different people in a progression of increasingly intrusive behavior. Identify what allowed you to reenter your cycle. It may be that you never saw your behavior as abusive in any way and thus saw no reason to stop. If you did feel that your behavior was wrong, what allowed you to go back to it? Explain how any of the following ideas that might apply to you: 1) If you have bad feelings after your offense, why were they not enough to prevent you from reoffending? 2) "Feeding the PIG" (the Problem of Immediate Gratification), 3) the attempt to fulfill unmet needs through your offending behavior or 4) editing your memory of the offense to make your behavior more acceptable.

Part Two: Your Personal Relapse Cycle

Use the diagram of "The Relapse Cycle" on page 5 in your *Relapse Prevention Workbook* to explain your personal cycle of offending. Study this diagram and a similar diagram attached to this guide, and describe in detail each phase of the cycle and how you have repeated the cycle. If you have had only one offense, describe how you moved from a "normal life" through stress to a high risk situation and finally to your offense. Put your cycle on a board in front of the class and explain each step.

Part Three: Relapse Prevention Strategies

You have a choice to complete this part of this task: The first choice is to complete all the assignments in the *Relapse Prevention Workbook for Sexually Compulsive Behaviors* by Dennis Daley and James Robert Ross (Learning Publications, 2000) workbook and hand in to your therapist. You may be asked to review certain parts of the *Workbook* with the group. If you have committed only one offense, describe your "relapse cycle" as it occurred for this one offense.

As an alternative, if you would like to complete a Christian faith-based relapse prevention strategy, you may choose to complete the assignments in the spiritually based workbook *Freedom from Sexually Compulsive Behavior*, which integrates relapse prevention strategies with the 12 steps. Because this is a more extensive workbook, you can use it to meet the requirements for an optional task as well as relapse prevention. Please let your therapist know if you want to use this alternative to you relapse prevention task.

Relapse Prevention Workbook

Dennis C. Daley, Ph.D.
and
J. Robert Ross, Ph.D.

ACKNOWLEDGMENTS: Thanks to the members of the sex offenders group led by J. Robert Ross, who have taught him much about the meaning of human sexuality and the importance of living in the truth, and to Dennis C. Daley, Ph.D., for his cooperation and suggestions in the revision of this workbook on relapse prevention for substance abuse problems, which was the inspiration for an application of relapse prevention principles to sexual compulsions.

TABLE OF CONTENTS

ONE - INTRODUCTION

Sexually compulsive behavior (SCB), also called sexual addiction, is a serious problem for many people. SCB can show in many different ways such as obsessive sexual fantasies, compulsive and excessive masturbation, use of pornography, multiple sex partners, anonymous or impersonal sex, phone or internet sex, or deviant and illegal sexual behavior. These behaviors often cause suffering for the affected individual and the family. In addition, SCB affects innocent victims and society as a whole, especially when it involves indecent public exposure, exploiting another person sexually, forced sex, hurting others with inappropriate sexual advances or behaviors, sex with children, or sex between two persons whose relationship is defined by a significant difference in power or authority--for example, between therapist and client, pastor and parishioner, teacher and student, etc.

Cybersex and the Porn Epidemic[2]

Although pornography, especially compulsive and addictive pornography use, is not the only way sexually compulsive behaviors manifest, porn use has skyrocketed in the past twenty-five years. It is now one of the major causes of marital distress.

How big is the porn business?
- More than 32 million different individuals visited a porn site in September of 2003.
- In 2008 this number had increased to 73 million visitors on average each month.
- The revenue generated by pornography exceeds the combined revenues of all professional football, baseball and basketball and is larger than the combined revenues of ABC, CBS and NBC.

How often do we view porn?
- Every second over $3,000 is spent on porn.
- Every second over 28,000 internet users are viewing pornography.
- Every second 372 internet users are typing adult, i.e., sex, search terms into search engines.
- Every 39 minutes a new pornographic video is being created in the United States.

What is the effect of pornography on marriage?
- increased callousness toward women
- devaluation of the importance of monogamy, decreased satisfaction with a partner's sexual performance, affection, and appearance
- doubts about the value of marriage

Are children into cybersex?

---

[2] Sources include: (1) *Adult Video News & Top Ten Reviews*, Inc. (2005); research by by Dolf Zillman and Jennings Bryant (1984, 1988); and the website http://internet-filter-review.toptenreviews.com/internet-pornography-statistics.html (Dec 12, 2010).

- 90% of 8-16 year olds view porn online, mostly while doing homework.
- 11 is the average age of first exposure to porn.
- 20%-30% of porn internet use is by children.
- 1 in 7 children each year receive a sexual solicitation online.

If pornography has become addictive or its use is causing problems in an intimate relationship, this workbook will be one important tool in the addict's recovery arsenal.

According to research and the clinical work of Dr. Patrick Carnes, a leading expert on sexual addiction or SCB is characterized by the following symptoms. These are adapted from symptoms of alcohol or drug dependence. Remember that you don't have to have all of these to have a serious problem with your sexual behavior:

- A pattern of out of control sexual behavior
- Severe consequences due to this behavior
- Trouble stopping despite negative consequences
- Persistent involvement in self-destructive or high risk behaviors
- Ongoing desire or efforts to limit your sexual behavior
- Sexual obsession or preoccupation
- Need to increase amount of sexual experience
- Severe mood changes around sexual activities
- Spending a lot of time on sexual activities or recovering from   them
- Neglecting important activities because of sexual behavior

Many problems and negative effects are associated with SCB. While many of these may result from SCB, some contribute to the sexual related problems. These include: (1) Physical problems such as spreading and acquiring sexually transmitted disease or HIV, being victimized by rape or other forms of violence, or physical injury to the genitals, breasts or colon as a result of certain sexual activities. (2) Emotional or psychological problems such as depression, hopelessness, despair, anxiety, fear, guilt, shame, loneliness, emptiness, or low self-esteem. (3) Family and relationship problems such as loss of relationships, damaged relationships, not fulfilling marital, parental or family responsibilities, separation, divorce, loss of children, domestic abuse, child abuse or neglect. In addition, family members may suffer much emotional pain such as deep anger, shame, despair, or depression. (4) Substance abuse (alcohol or other drugs) and psychiatric disorders such as mood disorders, impulse control disorders, and personality disorders. (5) Other problems related to work (e.g., loss of productivity, creativity, loss of job or career, or inability to keep a job), financial status (e.g., loss of income, heavy financial debts) or spirituality (e.g., feeling empty, shameful, cursed or bad).

Recovery from SCB is based on acceptance of your problem, a willingness to examine your specific behaviors and effects on you and others, and a desire to change.

When you start recovery from SCB, you will usually go through several different stages. The first stage involves making a decision to stop the behavior and making the commitment to a program of change. Some people struggle with this stage for years while others quickly make a decision to quit after something happens in their life that motivates them to change their sexual behavior. The second stage is actually quitting SCB, adjusting to living without the behavior, and dealing with the various issues faced in early recovery such as building a support system, identifying sexual triggers as well as strategies to manage these. The third stage is relapse prevention and refers to maintaining the positive gains you made over time in order to reduce the likelihood of relapse. In this stage, you continue to make changes in your attitudes, thinking, coping mechanisms, relationships, and lifestyle.

Although relapse may occur at any point in recovery, the greatest risk period is the first year. Within the first year, the first few months are the most difficult because your commitment may waver, you may have trouble adjusting to the interpersonal and mental changes that accompany a new lifestyle. Or, your lifestyle may pose numerous risks and pressures to staying free of destructive sexual behaviors. The purpose of this workbook is to help you and your family understand relapse as it relates to your SCB. This workbook will:

(1) Provide you with information on relapse and relapse prevention;

(2) Give you some practical ideas to reduce the chances of relapse;

(3) Help you identify specific high risk relapse factors that could lead to relapse;

(4) Help you begin to make specific relapse prevention plans based on your unique situation.

Throughout this workbook you will be asked to respond to questions and statements to assist you in devising your relapse prevention plan. This workbook is designed for use with other recovering persons, in individual or group counseling sessions, or with family members or a sponsor from Sex Addicts Anonymous (SAA) or another 12-step recovery group. If you are unable to resolve problems that may lead to a relapse either on your own or with the use of a 12-step group, seek help from a professional. You can get specific names from SAA friends or from your telephone directory.

TWO - UNDERSTANDING THE RELAPSE PROCESS

Relapse refers to the process of returning to a SCB such as going to a prostitute after a period of abstinence. Relapse is a possibility for you regardless of how much time your behavior has been under control. Part of your recovery plan should include learning about the relapse process and devising a plan to help prevent you from relapsing should warning signs of SCB occur.

Actual relapse is usually preceded by some period of negative pre-relapse changes in thoughts, fantasies, attitudes, mood or behavior. It is possible to build up to a relapse over a period of months. Or the build up to relapse may be very rapid, perhaps within a hour or so. Many sexually addicted persons have reviewed their relapse experiences and identified clues which preceded the relapse, which indicated they were headed back to using pornography or engaging in other destructive sexual behaviors.

Relapse clues, also called warning signs, refer to changes in your fantasies, behavior, attitudes, feelings, thoughts, or a combination of these. This does not necessarily mean that changes you experience are an indication that you must relapse. It simply means that you should be on the alert when changes occur so that you can examine whether or not these do in fact indicate that you may be headed for a relapse. Your clues may be very obvious, or they can be very subtle. The following are examples of "relapse clues" preceding relapses of others in recovery:

Behavior Changes

Increased irritability or episodes of arguing with others for no reason; a decrease in or stop in attendance at SAA meetings or counseling; reading personal ads, browsing through the X rated section of a video store or in an adult book store; cruising the Internet; cruising in your automobile without a specific destination in mind; increased symptoms of stress such as changes in eating or sleeping habits; lack of exercise; calling a 900 sex line; flirting with an illicit sex partner, or increased alcohol or drug use.

Attitude Changes

Not caring about SCB; not caring what happens to you; becoming negative about life and how things are going; believing you can recover on your own, or the opposite, believing that recovery is impossible.

Changes In Thoughts or Fantasies

Thinking you deserve a little sexual pleasure because you have not had any for several weeks or months; thinking it won't be any harm to substitute soft porn or an R rated movie for hard porn; thinking it's O.K. to have "just a friendly talk" with someone to whom you are attracted; fantasizing about an illicit sexual partner; or thinking that you deserve better than you are getting.

Changes In Feelings Or Moods
       Increased moodiness or depression; strong feelings of anger at oneself or another; increased feelings of boredom; or sudden feelings of euphoria.

These are just a few examples that may or may not relate to you. The important point to remember is that changes in your behaviors, attitudes, feelings, thoughts, fantasies or a combination of these could indicate that your relapse process is set in motion. The idea is to catch the early warning signs so that you can take quick action.

If you have experienced a period of recovery or after a period of abstinence from SCB, answer the following questions:

1.   What specific clues or warning signs preceded your relapse?

- _____

- _____

- _____

- _____

- _____

2. How much time elapsed between the emergence of your relapse clues and actual acting out sexually? _____
3.   Where did your relapse occur and who were you with at the time?

_____

1. If these were to occur again, what specific steps could you take to try to prevent a relapse?

- _____

- _____

- _____

- _____

- _____

THREE - IDENTIFYING HIGH RISK SITUATIONS

High risk situations include external and internal factors that increase your chances of engaging in one or more sexually compulsive behaviors. External factors include people, places, events and things that trigger your sexual compulsions. Internal factors include thoughts or feelings that make you want to escape into sexually compulsive behaviors. It is not the high risk factor in and of itself but your understanding of and willingness to implement appropriate relapse prevention strategies that determines whether you will relapse. (The New Testament teaches that God provides a way of escape from every temptation (1 Cor 10:13). If you have a faith in God or a Higher Power, one way to look at relapse prevention is to see it as learning about and using the way of escape that God offers you.)

An important relapse prevention strategy is to anticipate and plan ahead by identifying your individual high risk situations. You can then develop strategies to manage them so that you don't return to using pornography or engaging in inappropriate sexual behaviors.

The following list of potential high risk factors was identified by professionals, research studies and others who have experienced SCB or other types of addictions. Under each section, circle the number next to the high risk factor if you believe it applies to you. After you finish this task, you will be asked to identify two specific high risk factors, and develop a plan to manage these.

1. Upsetting Thoughts or Feelings or Difficulty Managing Feelings

N01	Anger expression problems (for example, holding anger in; expressing it inappropriately or violently).
N02	Anxiety or nervousness.
N03	Boredom or lack of constructive leisure interests.
N04	Depression.
N05	Fears which seem unreasonable.
N06	Feeling helpless or hopeless.
N07	Guilt.
N08	Feeling empty or feeling a lack of meaning in life
N09	Loneliness.
N10	Overconfidence ("I've got this think licked; I'll never use pornography again").
N11	Painful memories.
N12	Resentment towards others.
N13	Self-pity.
N14	Shame.

2. Sexually Stimulating Social Environment

S01	Being invited to a bachelor or stag party.
S02	Going to a strip joint by myself or with friends.
S03	Being around others who keep pornography and/or talk about sexual exploits.
S04	My social group consists mainly of others who use pornography or who have other sexually compulsive and destructive behaviors.

S05	Watching R or X rated movies or videos.
S06	Access to pornographic magazines or books.
S07	Access to sexual toys

3. Substance Use

A01	Using any alcohol.
A02	Using alcohol to excess.
A03	Using marijuana.
A04	Using speed or cocaine
A05	Using any other drugs (prescription or street drugs)

4. Internet Use

I01 Just going on-line.

I02 Going to chat rooms with sexual focus.

I03 Receiving e-mail or IM's with sexual content.

I04 Staying on-line after finishing school or work project.

I05 Surfing the net for pornographic sites.

5. Sobriety Plan Or Treatment-Related Problems

T01	Feeling that treatment is not helping me.
T02	I don't want to be involved in professional treatment.
T03	Change in motivation to stay in treatment.
T04	Impatience with recovery plan ("things are not happening fast enough").
T05	I seem to remain involved in recovery activities only for short periods of time.
T06	Missing my counseling or therapy session.
T07	Not going to SAA or other support group meetings regularly.
T08	Not working my individualized recovery plan (For example, not staying out of strip joints or staying off the internet, not completing my daily inventory; not working at making changes I agreed to as part of my recovery; etc.).

6. Problems In Relationships

R01	Not getting my family involved in my recovery.
R02	Arguing a lot with others.
R03	Difficulty meeting people not involved in SCB.
R04	Difficulty trusting others.
R05	I have no friends and tend to be a loner.
R06	My friends consist mainly of others who use pornography or have destructive sexual behaviors.
R07	Lack of sexual compatibility with spouse or partner.
R08	Serious conflicts or problems in a relationship.

7. Fantasies, Desires, Temptations, or Testing My Control

U01	Going to R or X rated movies.
U02	Having access to the internet in my home tempts me.

U03	I purposely put myself in sexually charged situations to see if I can avoid acting out.
U04	I sometimes get a desire for my SCB or act out without anything seeming to trigger this off.
U05	The sight of an attractive person sometimes triggers an urge to act out.
U06	The sight of certain places or things in my environment reminds me of using pornography and sometimes triggers an urge to act out.
U07	I fantasize or visualize a sexual act, person or situation.

8. Other High Risk Situations

O01	Achieving success at my job makes me want to reward myself.
O02	Difficulty handling evenings or weekends.
O03	Difficulty handling stress or anxiety.
O04	Difficulty solving problems without getting overwhelmed.
O05	Feeling good and happy about myself and my life.
O06	Lack of constructive ways of spending my days.
O07	Lack of hobbies or leisure time interests.
O08	Wanting to celebrate special occasions with sex (holidays, birthdays, etc.)
O09	Return of denial ("I don't have a sexual compulsion any longer").
O10	Excessive or impulsive behaviors (For example: drinking too much; gambling too much; overeating; spending too much money; overworking).
O11	Exhaustion or fatigue.
O12	Thinking I need pornography or sex in order to "have fun."
O13	Persistent negative thoughts about recovery, or my ability to change.
O14	Unusual or disturbing thoughts (hallucinations, paranoia).
O15	Others: _____

FOUR - STRATEGIES TO HANDLE HIGH RISK SITUATIONS

After you carefully review the list of high-risk relapse factors, go back to the ones you have marked. Choose two high-risk situations that you are concerned about now. Review all the facts related to each of these including all situation in your life, the thoughts and fantasies and everything you did including seemingly unimportant decisions that may have increased your risk of a relapse.

For example, Howard noted that he often became bored on weekends when he did not have any other activities planned. He would then spend time surfing the internet and end up viewing some pornographic web sites. Leonard noted that after he had an argument with his wife, he would begin fantasizing about a woman at work with whom he had flirted and who had indicated she might be interested in him. Heather, realized that when she was alone, she begin to fantasize about having illicit sex because it always made her feel wanted and loved.

For each of the two high-risk situation you identified, describe the specific facts related to the situation, and then write in two coping strategies or ways you can handle these situations without relapsing.

HIGH RISK SITUATION - 1 -- Related facts and information:_____

_____

_____

Coping Strategy 1: _____

Coping Strategy 2: _____

Coping Strategy 3: _____

HIGH RISK SITUATION - 2 -- Related facts and information:_____

_____

_____

Coping Strategy 1: _____

Coping Strategy 2: _____

Coping Strategy 3: _____

FIVE - IDENTIFYING AND HANDLING DESIRES OR CRAVINGS TO USE PORNOGRAPHY OR TO ACT OUT SEXUALLY

During the early months of recovery, it is common to experience fantasies, urges or cravings to use pornography or to act out sexually. Urges and cravings may differ in frequency and intensity with each person and may occur at any time even if you are actively involved in a recovery program. It is important to be aware of things that trigger an urge or craving, to look for physical and psychological signs or cravings, and to develop positive coping strategies.

Urges or cravings can be triggered by things you see in the environment that remind you of pornography or sex, internal discomfort such as anxiety or anger, or by things you don't seem to be able to identify. Physical signs may include tightness in your stomach, or feeling nervous throughout your body. Psychological signs may include increased thoughts of how good you feel when using pornography or engaging in other sexual behaviors.

Think of times when you have experienced strong desires for pornography or compulsive sex. What triggered your desire?

_____

What were the physical signs?

_____

What were the psychological signs?

_____

An important issue in the early stage of recovery--when you are not so used to handling your desires--is living with these without giving in to them. Desires normally decrease in frequency and severity as your recovery progresses. List below specific steps you can take to help you survive desires to engage in SCB:

1._____

2._____

3._____

4._____

Others who are recovering from sexual compulsions have used a number of practical methods to help them survive their sexual desires. These methods are listed below. Choose several that will help you handle urges to use pornography or to act out sexually.

- Talking With Others

    Talk with someone face-to-face or on the telephone such as a friend, family member, SAA/SCA sponsor, minister, or counselor. Attend an SAA/SCA meeting. If in counseling, request an appointment when your desires are overwhelming and you are worried about your ability to handle them. Keep names and telephone numbers in your wallet. Communicating helps put your conflict out in the open and will decrease the odds of acting on your desires.

- Redirecting Your Activity

    Get involved in an activity such as working around your home, or working out in some physical manner. Occupy yourself with reading. Write your thoughts and feelings in a journal. Get something to eat. Pray. Activities may take your mind off your desire. Physical activities help you relax.

- Surfing Your Cravings

    "Surfing your cravings" refers to the process of watching a build up of craving or sexual tension and just letting yourself feel it without any thought of getting relief by acting out. Tell yourself that you will just let yourself feel the craving instead of acting out or getting relief. Tell yourself that you can put off using pornography or acting sexually until tomorrow. Think of all the bad things that happened as a result of your behaviors. Think of how good you will feel if you do not slip. Think of all the benefits to you, both now and in the future; write these down on paper if needed. Think positively: "I'm not going to use" or "I will get through this urge or craving without acting out." Remember that the craving will not hurt you, but acting it out will destroy you. Repeat some of the recovery slogans such as "one day at a time," "easy does it," or "this too will pass."

- Avoiding Threatening Situations

    Don't go to bars, parties, events or clubs where you think it will be even more difficult to handle your sexual desires. Avoid socializing with others whom you feel may influence you to use pornography or act out sexually.

- Keeping A Daily Log

    Record each day in a log or on a calendar the overall degree to which you experienced desires to engage in SCB on a scale of 0 to 5 (0=not at all; 1=a fleeting thought; 2-3=moderate; 4=severe; 5=ready to relapse). When desires are rated 3 or above, list the circumstances in which they occurred, and list positive coping strategies that help you control them.

- Accountability Partner

    WHY: Experience has shown us that having an accountability partner is one of the most effective relapse prevention strategies. A trusted friend is a wall between myself and a temptation to do anything wrong or foolish, sexual or otherwise.

    WHAT: According to the Bible we need one another to help us with our bad behaviors. The Apostle encourages us: "My friends, if anyone is detected in a transgression, you who have received the Spirit should restore such a one in a spirit of gentleness. Take care that you yourselves are not tempted. Bear one another's burdens, and in this way you will fulfill the law of Christ" (Gal 6:1-2).

    Although this text addresses the needs of a person who has already fallen, there is an important application for the person who is tempted and before he makes a serious mistake. If we fail, we need an accountability partner to help restore us. We also need an accountability partner to help us not to fail to begin with.

In another place we read that we should, "encourage the fainthearted, help the weak, [and] be patient with all of them" (1 Thess 5:14). All of us are at one time or another "fainthearted" or "weak." We all need someone to encourage us and support us in the Christian life. That is what an accountability partner does.

WHO: Your accountability partner should be a person not closely related to you. He or she should not be your spouse. He should be a person of the same sex, someone you trust and who shares your values and will support your desire to avoid a SCB relapse.

HOW: You should have regular, weekly or at most every other week, meetings with your accountability partner. Although it is ok to socialize and shoot the breeze, the main purpose is to be open regarding your behavior relevant to your history of sexually compulsive behaviors. To help you do that your partner should use ask you the following questions. (These questions might be revised in some points to more closely match your unique issues and the way you might be tempted to act out sexually.)

Partners should take turns asking each other these questions. If any question is answered inappropriately, the partners should discuss what happened, why, and what can be done to avoid another incident of this kind.

In the last week have you:

1. Been exposed to any sexually explicit material?
2. Had any sexual thoughts about a person other than the partner with whom you live?
3. Engaged in any inappropriate conversation, or communication of any type with another person?
4. Engaged in flirtatious behavior, verbal or non-verbal?
5. Been with someone in a way that was inappropriate or showed a lack of good judgment?
6. Watched any image whether by print, video, TV, or internet that could be described as hard porn (total nudity)?
7. Watched any image whether by print, video, TV, or internet that could be described as hard porn (partial nudity presented in a sexually suggestive manner)?
8. Engaged in masturbation using either pornography or a fantasy of another person?
9. Spent fifteen minutes each day in contemplation, reading recovery materials or some material that would support your spiritual life?
10. Been responsible in all of your financial transactions?
11. Have you lied to your family or friends?
12. Have you just lied to me?

SIX - IDENTIFYING AND HANDLING
BIOLOGICAL, SOCIAL AND CULTURAL INFLUENCES

Sexually explicit images and examples of destructive sexual behavior are easy to find and difficult to avoid. These images appear in print, on TV, videos, movies and on many sites on the Internet. In addition, our culture is saturated with sexually suggestive messages, which reach us in popular music, movies, television, and advertising. These media bombard us daily with messages that address and activate our sexual instincts and promote many of our sexual fantasies. Your own pattern of sexually compulsive behaviors has probably fixated your normal, healthy sexual feelings so that it is very difficulty to use sex in healthy rather than destructive ways. Successful recovery depends upon recognizing and finding ways to handle normal sexual instincts that have become fixated on destructive patterns of behavior and on strategies to handle the social and cultural influences that help perpetuate your destructive fantasies.

1. First, identify and describe your usual, not necessarily deviant, sexual feelings and how they are reflected in your fantasy life. When I have sexual feelings or feel aroused I often have the following thoughts or fantasies:

- _____

- _____

- _____

2. How will these fantasies affect your thoughts and feelings, and to what behavior are they likely to lead?

Example: Your Thoughts are:

_____

_____

Your Feelings are:

_____

_____

Your Potential Behaviors are: _____

_____

3. Identify at least three powerful, sexually suggestive messages in the culture around you and describe how you think they may pose a threat to your recovery:

Examples:

_____

_____

_____

4. After you identify these messages and the threat they pose to your recovery, describe specific, concrete behaviors--things you can do to help you cope without falling back into your destructive, compulsive sexual behavior.

_____

_____

_____

Some of the common social and cultural pressures experienced by recovering persons were listed earlier in the section on high risk situations (units 3 & 4). There are many other situations that you may experience in recovery that put you at risk for a relapse. These may include any of the following: (1) access to the Internet, (2) working or socializing with others who read or keep pornography, (3) working or socializing with someone who gives you a message that says, "I am available," (4) access to soft porn movie channels on television, and (5) regular TV programs with sexual content or seductive images in popular print and (6) advertising.

Review the following ways others have handled these sexual messages in our culture and mark those that will be of use to you:

___ Have blocks placed on pornographic Internet sites.
___ Politely avoid social contact with anyone engaging you in a sexually suggestive conversation.
___ Cancel cable service to the Playboy channel and other porn channels
___ Report regularly to your SAA/SCA sponsor your contact with any sexually suggestive material and the fantasies activated by this material.
___ Avoid X rated moves--and R rated movies with sexually explicit content.

If you feel anxious or sexually stimulated or begin to experience destructive sexual fantasies, then you should leave the environment. As soon as possible, arrange a time to discuss this high-risk situation with your SAA/SCA sponsor or your counselor.

SEVEN - ANGER MANAGEMENT IN RECOVERY

Many people in recovery attribute their relapses to an inability to constructively handle anger. Mismanaged anger poses a threat to your recovery; it can also lead to problems in resentment and relationships with others. Anger refers to negative feelings such as frustration or resentment as well as more obvious expressions of anger such as yelling or getting violent.

Some experts believe that unresolved resentment and anger is the single greatest cause of relapses for many kinds of compulsive behavior, including SCB. If, over a period of time, you feel hurt and resentful, you will inevitably begin to think that you have a right to some fun. And that means you are already rationalizing in your mind that you have a "right" to act out sexually.

Anger is normal. It is not wrong. But it is hazardous to your spiritual health, and you must deal with it constructively, or it will blow up in your face in the form of SCB. The following steps may help you learn to understand, recognize and deal with anger in constructive ways:

Step 1.   Recognize Angry Feelings.

Be aware of when you are angry or beginning to feel resentment. How does your anger show? Look for anger clues. Physical signs may include headaches, tension in your stomach, or rapid speech. Psychological signs may include revenge fantasies, increased thoughts of SCB, or feeling depressed. Behavioral signs may include increased argumentativeness with others, intentionally avoiding others, or showing aggressive behaviors in your interactions with others.

List below your typical signs of anger and resentment:

Physical signs:_____

_____

_____

Psychological signs: _____

_____

_____

Behavioral signs: _____

_____

_____

Step 2. Identify Possible Causes Of Your Anger Or Resentment.

Examine all the contributing factors related to your anger or resentment by identifying the situation that triggered your anger, who else is involved, and why you feel anger now.

List below the causes of your anger or resentment:

_____

_____

_____

Step 3. Identify Effects Of Your Anger On Self And Others.

Examine your usual responses to your angry feelings. Do you do nothing and allow anger to build up inside? Do you lash out at others and get into arguments or fights? Do you try to ignore the situation or your angry feelings? Do you talk about your anger?

List below how you usually handle angry feelings.

_____

_____

_____

How does your method of handling your anger affect you?

_____

_____

_____

How does your method of handling anger affect others?

_____

_____

_____

Step 4. Decide On The Best Method Of Handling Your Anger.

a. Decide first if your anger is really justified. It may be an overreaction to a situation or a result of self-anger, which you misplace on others. If your anger doesn't seem justified, talk yourself out of it by changing your beliefs or thoughts.

b. Talk directly to the person with whom you are angry. Be calm, respectful, and specific about your feelings.

c. Talk to a third party in order to release your feelings and gain a better understanding of the situation that has you angry.

d. Direct angry feelings towards constructive activities--for example, jogging, working around your home, or other physical activities.

e. Change your thoughts For example, change "I'm angry at you because...," to "it's unfortunate this happened but I don't have to feel angry."

f. Do not allow anger to build up. Complete an "anger check" at the end of each day to insure you are not allowing your anger or resentments to build up.

Step 5. Anticipate The Outcome Of Your Chosen Method To Handle Your Anger.

Of the alternatives you have at this time, which seems the most appropriate for the current situation? What is likely to happen if you choose and implement this particular alternative? What will you do if this does not work in helping you resolve your anger?

If you are chronically angry at others or have lingering resentment, if you still have difficulty handling anger or resentments after trying the previously mentioned ideas, or if you have trouble using ideas learned in the SAA or SCA program, you must seek help with a professional to learn more appropriate and useful anger management techniques before your anger leaks out in SCB.

EIGHT - USE OF LEISURE TIME IN RECOVERY

One of the issues facing every recovering person is learning to use constructively free or leisure time. When you give up using pornography or acting out sexually you must find new replacements. You cannot afford to allow boredom and a lack of constructive activities to give you reason to return to pornography or destructive sex.

Think of the most difficult times of the day and week for you. List these below in order from most to least difficult:

1._____

2._____

3._____

4._____

List leisure activities you have enjoyed in the past (that don't center around pornography or sex):

1._____

2._____

3._____

4._____

List any activities which you have curtailed or given up due to your sexual addiction:

1._____

2._____

3._____

4._____

List those activities in which you will continue to participate during your ongoing recovery program:

1._____

2._____

3._____

4._____

List several new leisure time activities you would like in your ongoing recovery:

1._____

2._____

3._____

4._____

List four reasons why it is important for your recovery to have constructive leisure activities.

1._____

2._____

3._____

4._____

People sometimes prevent themselves from following through with their plans, creating their own barriers to recovery. List how you might prevent yourself from following through with your leisure time activities:

1._____

2._____

3._____

NINE - BUILDING A LONG-TERM RECOVERY PLAN

To continue working at your recovery, it is important to have a specific plan to follow after completing any professional treatment program for your sexual compulsion. This plan involves identifying specific steps to take in order not to use SCB, changes you need to make, and recovery resources you will use to maintain your recovery.

It is important to accept the fact that recovery is a long-term, painful process requiring you to take a close look at yourself. Below is a list of recovery resources to help in your continued work towards recovery. Check the ones you feel you need at this time. It is a good idea to review these with another person who is familiar with your sexual compulsions.

1. Outpatient counseling for self and/or family.

Date of appointment: _____ Place: _____

2. SAA/SCA/Other Recovery Meetings. Number of times each week: ___

    Location   Day/Time of Meeting

_____   _____

_____   _____

3. Finding an SAA/SCA sponsor by: _____

4. Working The SAA/SCA Twelve Step Program starting on_____

5. Reading Recovery Literature--be specific: _____
_____(See the list of resources at the end of this booklet.)

6. Other--List other specific steps will you take to help you continue in recovery and resolve your problems:

(1) _____

(2) _____

TEN - LIFESTYLE BALANCING AND RECOVERY

Recovery from sexually compulsive behaviors requires you to make significant changes in your life. The specific areas you change will depend on your unique situation. Healthy recovery involves a reasonable balance in the different areas of your life. Review the following areas to determine which ones you may need to change:

- **Continued Recovery**

  Plan for continued involvement in recovery for your pornography and/or sexually compulsive behaviors. This includes participation in SAA/SCA, counseling or other special services. Your family should also be involved as needed. Include steps to stay motivated to change.

- **Physical Health**

  Maintain your physical health through proper nutrition and eating habits, physical exercise and proper rest as well as regular physical examinations.

- **Recreation/Leisure**

  Constructive interests that do not evolve around pornography or sex need to be a regular part of your life. You need to have fun and enjoy a variety of recreational and social activities, alone as well as with others.

- **Relationships**

  When possible, make amends to people you have hurt as a result of your sexually compulsive behaviors. (It is advised that you consult with an SAA/SCA sponsor or your counselor on the best way to make appropriate amends for destructive behaviors). Cultivate and nurture nonsexual relationships with family members, friends, and others. Avoid relationships that may have been connected in any way with your previous sexually destructive behaviors.

- **Work Or School**

  Develop occupational or educational goals suited to your abilities and interests. Don't spend excessive time at work at the expense of other areas of your life.

- **Spirituality**

  Maintain your unique relationship with God or your "higher power." Use meditation or prayer by participating in your religious faith. Seek out a religious community that will support your recovery.

- **Psychological Health**

  Improve how you feel about yourself by making positive changes in yourself, changing negative thought patterns or negative behavior patterns, expressing your feelings to others in appropriate ways, and coping with stress in positive ways. Reward yourself for maintaining your recovery. Take regular inventories of your strengths and weaknesses to determine which areas you need to change.

Discuss with your SAA/SCA sponsor, counselor or pastor the shame connected to your sexual compulsions. Learn to develop a healthy, positive view of your sexuality including an acceptance of the power of your sexual feelings. Develop a healthy view of sexual relations, which includes respect for your sexual partner as a real person in his/her own right.

● **Financial Health**

Take care of your debts and resolve financial problems, and use your money wisely. Get rid of credit cards. Develop a budget and a plan for saving. Don't squander all of your money now–save for the future.

Review each of these eight areas as they relate to your life at the present time. Which areas are out of balance and need work? List below two areas that you feel you need to begin changing and three specific steps you can take to begin this process:

Lifestyle Change:_____ In order to make this change I will:
- _____
- _____
- _____

Lifestyle Change:_____ In order to make this change I will:
- _____
- _____
- _____

ELEVEN- EMERGENCY RECOVERY CARD

Carry an "emergency recovery card" in your wallet or purse that lists names and telephone numbers of others who are concerned with helping you maintain your recovery. When you feel your recovery is threatened, that is the time to rely on your recovery card. List three people you can call on and their telephone numbers.

Name   Phone Number

_____   _____

_____   _____

_____   _____

If you do not have a list of supportive people to rely on when things get rough, develop a network of reliable friends over the next several months. Use contacts in SAA or SCA.

TWELVE - WHAT TO DO IF A RELAPSE OCCURS

You plan not to relapse, but if you should engage in a destructive, compulsive behavior, you must convince yourself to stop immediately. As soon as possible discuss your SCB slip with a concerned person such as a family member, SAA/SCA sponsor, counselor, minister, or friend.

You can anticipate feeling guilty and disappointed after relapsing. Don't allow these feelings to give you permission to continue your compulsive behavior.

If you have acted out sexually over a period of time, longer than a few days, and can't stop on your own, then seek professional help. If you relapse after quitting or reducing treatment activities, you should return to treatment again. Contact your counselor, or if you do not have a counselor, contact SAA or SCA or your local mental health clinic, physician, or clergy person and ask for a referral to a professional who is experienced in helping people with sexually compulsive behaviors.

You can also contact SAA/SCA sponsors or friends who may help you return to working a recovery plan. In some instances, a return to SAA/SCA programs will provide you with enough help and support to get back into recovery. In other cases professional counseling or group treatment may be needed. The main issue is for you to stop the relapse as soon as possible--before it gets out of hand.

THIRTEEN - DAILY RELAPSE PREVENTION INVENTORY

Recovery is a daily process. At the end of each day, take time to review the following questions:

Were there any clues present today indicating that you are building up to act out a sexually compulsive behavior?

Have you had any fantasies of a sexually destructive behavior?

What are your most recent scores on your craving log? Are there any 3's, 4's, or 5's (See Section 5, "Keeping a Craving Log")?

Did you experience any high-risk situations today that could trigger off a relapse if you don't take action now?

If you answered yes to any of these questions, what is your plan to help reduce the chances of a relapse: Write this plan below:

_____

_____

FOURTEEN - SUMMARY OF RECOVERY AND RELAPSE PREVENTION STRATEGIES

As you continue to work at making positive changes in your life, you will experience many of the benefits of recovery. Keep working hard! Use the following strategies to help you prevent a relapse.

1. Work a disciplined recovery program. Consistency, hard work and discipline are keys to successful recovery.

2. Don't try to recover alone. Seek support and help from other men and women in recovery, professionals, friends and family. Don't keep secrets and share your struggles and conflicts.

3. Develop healthy relationships with positive people. Focus on non-sexual aspects of these relationships.

4. Accept the ups and downs of recovery. You may have strong desires, bad days, and lose motivation. Accept these as normal and have a plan to help you through the rough spots.

5. Be prepared for people, places, events and things that can influence you to act out. Know when to avoid certain situations and practice different ways to change strong sexual fantasies.

6. Learn to manage your feelings. Don't let anger, anxiety, boredom, depression, guilt, shame, or loneliness give you a reason to stop recovery or act out.

7. Learn to change negative thoughts and compulsive sexual fantasies. Challenge your thinking when it becomes negative. Practice this daily so you decrease negative and increase positive thoughts.

8. Remember the problems caused by your compulsion. Remind yourself of the short and long-term benefits of recovery.

9. Keep busy and have fun. Build non-sexual- related activities into your life.

10. Don't let yourself be taken off guard if you experience any setback in your life.

11. Appreciate and reward your efforts at recovery. Don't take yourself for granted and don't overlook positive change, no matter how small.

12. Know the warning signs of relapse. Early recognition is essential if you are to catch problems early before things get out of control.

13. Know your high risk relapse factors. This will enable you to develop practical strategies to lower relapse risk.

14. Continue to regularly take an inventory of yourself. Self-examination leads to increased self-awareness which in turn helps you decide what to change.

15. Attend support group meetings, get a sponsor, and use the tools of recovery from sexual addictions and compulsions. You can access several resources on the Internet including the following:

- Sex Compulsion Anonymous (SCA) www.sca-recovery.org
    NOTE: SCA has online meetings closed to the general public. For more information about these meetings and how you might participate, go online at: www.sca-recovery.org/closed.html.
- Sex Addicts Anonymous (SAA) email address info@saa-recovery.org
- Sex and Love Addicts Anonymous (SLAA)email SLAAfws@aol.com
- Sexaholics Anonymous (SA) email saico@sa.org
- Sexual Recovery Anonymous email 103427.356@compuserve.com

16. Focus on your spirituality and personal growth.

17. Get help with other addictions or mental health problems.

Relapse Prevention – Part Four: Three Steps to Healthy Coping

Discuss the meaning of the following steps to healthy coping and explain how you will implement each step in order to prevent a relapse:

Step One: Identify the risk. What are your personal warning signs and high risk situations?

Step Two: Take action. Upon recognizing a risky situation, immediately leave the high risk situation, or call someone to discuss the situation, and/or implement one or more of your other relapse prevention strategies.

Step Three: Take your inventory. After leaving the situation reflect on the following questions:

- Would this behavior be just a small slip?
- Can I give myself at least an hour before acting?
- Do I want to hurt someone I love?
- What kind of person do I want to be?
- How is my life better now than it used to be?
- What could I lose if I act on this feeling?
- What are my blessings? Count at least ten.
- What are ten good things about me?
- What need am I trying to meet when I have an urge to act out
- How can I meet this need in a better, more healthy way?
- Who will I talk to about the activity or situation I was in and my temptation to slip?
- What was I thinking that made it possible for you to consider committing a sexual offense. Analyze, discuss and correct this faulty thinking.

Finally, remember that the "road to hell is paved with good intentions." Going through your relapse prevention task will not actually prevent a relapse unless you execute the strategies you have developed to prevent a relapse and never commit another sex offense. You must follow through using what you learned in the *Relapse Prevention Workbook*

_____

THERAPY TASKS V and VI
Optional Tasks

Each client must complete two optional tasks (only one if you completed *Freedom from Sexually Compulsive Behavior*). Below are a list of possible optional tasks. In choosing your optional tasks ask yourself, "What is there about my life that needs to improve, and what would I like to work while I am in this program?"

Instructions for Optional Tasks

1. Define the issue or problem in your life. Be as specific as possible.

2. Specify the goal of this project. What you would like to see happen to make your life better? Be specific. Don't give a vague answer such as, "I would like to be happy."

3. Describe the exact steps you will begin taking to make this happen. Be very specific, e.g. "I will see a marriage counselor once a week beginning August 1"; or "I will make a budget and live by it beginning Aug 1;" or something similar just as specific.

4. What questions or concerns do you have about how to achieve your goal.

Descriptions of Some Optional Tasks

Optional Task: Reconnecting with People and the Community

Many sexual offenders experience isolation and withdrawal after parole from prison or upon receiving a probated sentence. Isolation is a dangerous warning sign and should be confronted immediately. How did you previously isolate yourself while in your cycle? What problems have you encountered in your efforts to connect with your family and the community? How do you plan to resolve these difficulties?

Present your plans for reintegrating into the community and breaking the cycle of isolation by answering the following questions. Be specific. Your answers should include "what, when, where and how."

1. How has your offense or incarceration negatively affected your relationships with your family, your friends, your employer, your church, and your neighbors?

2. How and where will you meet people to expand your social/support network?

3. What are your doing to build a good relationship with your family?

4. How will you relate to an intimate partner, if any?

5. Describe your current life style. How balanced is it socially, physically, vocationally, recreationally and spiritually? Review again the part of the *Relapse Prevention Workbook* that relates to development of a balanced lifestyle.

Optional Task: Anger Management

Discuss the important and powerful role anger has played in your life.

(1) Describe how anger surfaces in your daily life. State whether you think your family, friends, and others in the group see you as angry and ways you display it or hide and minimize your anger.

(2) How is anger related to feeling threatened or put down?

(3) How does anger seem to help you control situations, people and feelings of low self-esteem?

(4) How did anger or resentment contribute to your offense(s).

(5) Anger is always a secondary emotion. Underneath are always other feelings such as hurt or disappointment. What feelings lie beneath your anger. How do you like these feelings? What do you do with them? Reveal them or hide them? Why?

(6) Finally, use the ***Anger Management Exercise*** available from Anchor Counseling to answer other questions regarding your use of anger and strategies to handle it more effectively.

Optional Task: Healing for Yourself as a Victim of Abuse

One of the most damaging aspects of abuse is the secrecy that surrounds it. Secrecy increases feelings of shame, low self esteem, and isolation. Part of healing is breaking through the silence and talking about what happened to you.

Prepare and present your personal history of victimization. Share those incidents where you were the victim of physical, emotional, and sexual abuse or neglect. In what ways did you blame yourself? How did you bury your shame about what happened? What other feelings are you aware of as you talk about your victimization? How does getting in touch with your feelings of being a victim help you to better understand the pain and damage experienced by the person you molested?

Decide if it would be helpful to enter personal therapy to deal with the issues from your previous victimization.

Another Personalized Treatment Project for Your Optional Task

If you wish to work on another issue in your life, for example, low self esteem, depression, social skills, nicotine addiction, marital or family issues, please make a proposal to work on a personalized treatment project. You must present your proposal your personalized task to the group for approval.

THERAPY TASK VII: Restitution

You must develop a plan of restitution that offers some of your personal resources for the benefit of others. However, before you implement your restitution you must present your plan and have it approved by the group before you begin.. Some examples of restitution include:

1. Agree to meet with and assist new clients in treatment who are unable to break through denial and admit their offense.

2. Agree to meet with a new group and assist them in understanding and assuming ownership of their offense by presenting your own offense story.

3. Agree to present to a college class, juvenile sex offenders or another approved group interested in understanding sexual abuse and its impact on victim.

4. At the request of your victim's therapist, agree to participate in treatment aimed at healing your victims. Your participation must likewise have the endorsement of the Sex Offender Treatment Team.

5. Make a financial contribution to an agency that treats victims of sexual abuse or another agency that helps other people.

6. Agree to participate in some other form of restitution that you develop through your personal initiatives.

Therapy Task VIII – Shame Resiliency

Based upon readings from the book, *Healing the Shame that Binds You* by John Bradshaw

Instructions: First, read and study the specific sections assigned in each chapter of the book. Second, answer the questions assigned for each chapter. Third, discuss your answers with the group.

One: Understanding Shame, pp. 7-8

Assignments

1. Write your definition of shame:

2. Check all of the ways you feel shame: ___ Rejected, ___ Failure ___ Defective, ___ Soft (not tough), ___ Ridiculed, ___ Unworthy

3. How can shame be good and healthy?

Two: Toxic or Unhealthy Shame

• Neurotic Syndromes of Shame, p. 29-30

• Shame as Self-Alienation, pp. 33-34

• Shame as the Core and Fuel of All Addiction, pp. 35-36

• Sexual Abuse, pp. 40-41

• Shame as Hopelessness-The Squirrel Cage, pp. 42-43

Assignments

1. Do you try to hide the real you from others? Why?

2. Define the word "alien."

3. How does shame make you an alien?

4. Do you experience shame because of your sex offense? If so, explain how it might promote even more destructive behavior.

5. Do you believe that you can never recover from your shame? Why or why not?

Three: The Major Sources of Toxic Shame

• The Family System, pp 45-46

• Max's Story, pp. 47-50

• Sexual Abuse, pp 72-75

Assignments

1. How has your family shamed you?

2. Describe the shame you feel about your sex offense(s)

3. In what other ways have you been shamed?

4. When you are shamed how does it feel like physically (in your body)?

5. What are your symptoms of shame?

Four Part A: The Hiding Places of Toxic Shame, pp. 121-129

- Striving for Power and Control
- Rage
- Arrogance or Pride
- Criticism and Blame
- Judgementalism and Moralizing
- Contempt (Disgust)
- Patronizing
- Caregiving and Helping
- People-Pleasing and Being Nice
- Envy
- Compulsive/Addictive Behaviors
  Assignments

1. Pages 121-129 describe several ways we try to hide or defend ourselves against our shame. Describe how you have used at least three of the ways of hiding shame in your own life.

2. Does hiding your shame really help? Why or why not?

Four Part B: Reenactments, Reenacting Victimization, Criminal Behavior, pp. 144-147

3. What is a re-enactment of a shame event?

4. Why would a victim want to re-enact his or her victimization?

5. Jurgen Bartsch (pp 144-147) was himself a victim, who became an offender. Were you ever a victim in any way? If yes, do you see any connection between your victimization and your offense(s)?

Five: Coming our of Hiding and Isolation

- Finding a Social Network, pp 153-156
- Guidelines for Selecting a Group, pp 156-157.
  Assignments

1. Which of the following do you experience when feel shame?

    ___ Disconnected from others

    ___ Not as good as others

    ___ Like I don't belong in the group

    ___ Like I want to hide

2. There are three ways to hide or to defend ourselves when we feel shame: (1) move away and withdraw from others, or (2) move against others aggressively, or (3) move toward others in an attempt to appease them or make them like us. Which of these do you use most often to defend from shame?

3. In order to recover from shame why is it important to be a part of a group that knows you, including your sex offense(s)?

4. When you share something that makes your vulnerable, do you like for the other person to...

___ Make eye contact?

___ Look away?

___ Give me a you a hug?

___ Just listen carefully to everything?

5. What other response would you like from the person with whom you are sharing?

Six: Confronting and Changing Your Toxic Inner Voices

- The Inner Voice As Automatic Thoughts, p 203
- Stopping Obsessive Shaming Thoughts, pp 208-212

Assignment: Discuss with the group how it helps you to follow the steps on pp 210-212 to stop your toxic inner voices.

Seven: Choosing To Love and Forgive Yourself for Your Mistakes

- Reframing Mistakes, p 229
- Mistakes as Warnings, p 229
- Mistakes as Allowing Spontaneity, p 230
- Mistakes as Teachers, p 230
- Common Categories of Mistakes, pp 231-232
- The Habit of Awareness, p 233

Assignments

1. Explain why it is OK to make mistakes.

2. Try developing the habit of awareness using the questions on p. 233. Does this help you make fewer mistakes? How?

Concluding Assignment: Tell the group how they might be able to help, or how they have already helped, you recover from your shame.

THERAPY TASK IX - Final Group Review

Part One: Post-Treatment/Pre-Release Test

Name_____ Date_____

Which of the following are good strategies to prevent a relapse? Check all that apply.

1._____ talking with a trusted person who understands your problem and will support your relapse prevention plan.

2._____ engage in a positive, constructive behavior.

3._____ talk to the person about whom you are having deviant fantasies.

4._____ surf your deviant sexual desires

5._____ avoid high risk situations

6._____ maintain a daily log to track deviant desires and fantasies.

7._____ meet with an accountability partner regularly

8._____ use pornography to satisfy sexual desires

Answer True (T) or False (F):

9._____ Self destructive behaviors tend to repeat in a cyclical pattern with certain identifiable precursors to the offense.

10. _____ A relapse/reoffending usually happens without any warning signs

11. _____ The prevention of a relapse begins with the identification of my unique high risk situations and relapse triggers.

12._____ The best way to avoid a relapse is to just be determined not to let it happen again.

13. _____ Resentment and anger do not often have anything to do with my committing an offense.

14._____ Relapse prevention should include the development of a well rounded plan to live a balanced healthy life style including one's physical health, recreation and leisure, family and social relationships, work or school, spiritual life, financial affairs, and a healthy sexuality.

15._____ Depending upon the extent and nature of previous offenses, a regular relapse prevention inventory should be taken daily, weekly or monthly, preferably with a support person.

16. _____ Specific, concrete behavioral strategies should be devised to respond to each high risk situation so as to avoid a relapse.

17. Explain the difference between "control my deviant sexual fantasies" and "cure my deviant sexual fantasies."

18. What factors in your past do you think contributed to your sexually abusing someone?

19. Review each of the treatment objectives (page xxx) and explain how you have or have not achieved each objectives

20. In your own words, describe how you think treatment has helped you.

21. List the personal strengths you have that will assist you in the future to avoid re-offending..

22. How has your thinking about sex changed during your treatment?

23. Finally, what do you appreciate most about your treatment program, and what part of it was the least helpful to you?

Part Two: Answer the following questions:

(1) Describe in detail and present to the group a review of all your treatment tasks and what you have learned from them

(2) Describe your personal Relapse Prevention Plan with specific strategies you will use to avoid a relapse or another offense.

(3) Describe your present family situation and describe what you are doing to rebuild a strong relationship with your spouse and/or children.

(4) Finally, tell each person in the group how they have helped you and have contributed to your recovery.

Additional Resources

Carnes, Patrick. *Contrary to Love: Helping the Sexual Addict.* Hazelden, 1989.

Hession, Roy. *The Calvary Road* CLC Publications, Fort Washington, PA, 1950.

Linn, Jan G. *Living Inside Out: Learning How To Pray the Serenity Prayer.* Chalice Press, St. Louis, MO, 1994.

Miller, Keith. *Hunger for Healing: The Twelve Steps as a Classic Model for Christian Spiritual Growth.* San Francisco: Harper, 1992.

Ross, James Robert. *Freedom from Sexually Compulsive Behaviors* (2013). Available from Amazon.com.